Caroline Teague is a London bor[...] on grief, identity and how the[...] harrowing realities of being hum[...] they call 'tragic optimism' hoping[...] writing can translate into something positive and comforting for someone else.

Creator of the musical project "Caroline Smiling" which blends music, spoken word and illustration to creatively communicate ideas around mental health and queer identity. Caroline was the international guest at the Portugal Slam in Lisbon in October 2018 and the poet in residence at the Stanza poetry festival in St. Andrews, Scotland in March 2019, continuing to perform their work regularly at poetry and literary events across the UK, including venues such as the Royal Albert Hall, the Royal Festival hall, the Roundhouse and the Arnolfini theatre in Bristol.

They also curate London's only regular 3-round Slam, Genesis Poetry Slam, and is an artist-in-residence at the Vauxhall-based queer cabaret night Bar Wotever.

GOOD EARTH

Caroline Teague

Burning Eye

BurningEyeBooks
Never Knowingly
Mainstream

This edition published by Burning Eye Books 2019

www.burningeye.co.uk

@burningeyebooks

Burning Eye Books
15 West Hill, Portishead, BS20 6LG

ISBN 978-1-911570-77-6

"For all the people with heavy hearts and hopeful heads"

Contents

To Sea! To Sea!

A man comes into the shop I work in.
Touches my hair without permission.

On the ride home the newspaper tells me
that I cry too much and that black people
are still responsible for their own murders.

At night, I lay my scarf-wrapped head down and dream of
being broken-backed on a boat somewhere, sailing but still not
knowing how to navigate my way through these hostile waters.

*

Lonesome ships of broad timber
cut through furious waves
                    slashing at the sides of our bows
seas they joke that we don't know how to

swim in, brimming with sharp angry white sharks
          the people of industry poke

holes in
                    our undersides

curse us for letting in the ocean, blame us for it making us salty
when the storm comes, the things
          that have been breathing easy
underwater chuckle

deep inhales of blue lung air
          dislodge their jaws, waiting for us to

                    capsize

mouths wide and with full bellies they lick their lips
telling each other

Their captains were corrupted! Of course they were going to
drown when they didn't teach each other how to swim!

when we didn't bring ourselves out to sea
      children of the sun
         we were dragged into their Atlantics
              the ones that no one can own
           but somehow belong to them, on vessels not
         of our design

                  missing the feel of the earth
                  beneath our feet.

*

In the morning, I wake soaked and gasping.
Fall out of the dry drowning of the bed quickly,
realise I am not drenched in the ocean I had been
dreaming was killing me.

Dressing for the day, the radio stream scolds me for adding to
the numbers. The house is still cold from the stories of saviours
on public transport. The silence of no one asking how brown
girl is doing.
A girl at work puts her fingers in my hair and tells me how lucky
black girls are. Something inside my chest feels like a seashell
and I pull it out and up to my ear and hear it crying out

To sea!
                To sea!

Monochrome

One morning I had a dream that a friend I lost back to the universe came to tell me that the sun was never going to rise again.

> On a commute to work pressing me, lifeless fruit, I shudder. Shoulder to shoulder with bruised peaches and angry apples.
>
> The sky hangs, still dark, over the city and I start to cry when we get into central London.
>
> I know it should be some small kindness
> to know that after people have gone
> the earth still orbits.

The sun was staring at me through the glass window but I still couldn't shake off the surety that I was never going to see it again.

Brown Sugar on White Canvas

No matter the blend you are dark oil paint,
beautiful little sugar girl.
You are your mother's favourite.
She calls you pudding still.
Rubs your cheeks and you feel your brown
become sweet under her soft dark hands.

You have been taught that no one can tell you
how to love your tone.
There will be times when you may wobble
above the borrow of a black beauty,
below the mark of an ice queen.
You hear extended family talk about what it is
to be the spoilt blood of the tar man
and the white devil. You exhale.

Snow-white face of your friend will laugh at you, tell you not to
    try to understand
what it is to be brown across the sea.
Arctic fox you used to know and love
will chase you halfway home,
howling into the sky that you are wrong.
When you know you are meant to smile,
laugh and stay docile.

You the rabbit.
                You the prey.

You who can speak of being equal,
but so long as you speak of equality
in this way.
Do not become teary.

They do not know of running their night out
with animal calls that they are made
more of monkey than of man.
You look for a way to make them understand

that even if you will have been called nigger
less than your mother

it is still once enough too many times.

Your gorgeous Irish flower wept for you
in a police station swollen with men.
Recorded the detail, how much it may have hurt
in ink and programme.
Small pink sting below the left cheek
that would later look like a sarcastic rose
blooming in the mirror.

Do not weep, whatever you do.
Don't go home for a week.
Do not tell your mother a man leapt forward
furious,
wanting to beat the black out of you
that you inherited from her.

A slap.
A grudge.
A hiss from a stranger.
Asking which one of your parents
was the nigger lover.
A chase.
A hit.
Not one piece of this is new,
yet still when you open your mouth to talk
your city will roll its eyes,
tell you we are all one underneath.

Don't cry, whatever you do.
Like it really is a molehill,
not the mountain that you have been halfway
stuck on your whole life.

Your coarse hair
a wreath to be tugged and tamed.

Your face
a paint-by-numbers canvas,
confusing.
Your body
a junkyard of wishful thinking.
Your womb
the potential graveyard
for the child you are still too heartbroken
to bring, unsuspecting, into a world like this.

You curse yourself as if you are already a ghost.

But aren't you the beautiful little sugar girl?
Remember you are still your mother's favourite.
She calls you pudding, still.
You are more than paint,
                    than dessert.

Five-Year-Late Eulogy

It was so strangely beautiful watching you slowly disappear. The way you melted off the face of this earth, the peel and slip of ice from a glass bottle. In lucid sleepwalking I would remove things from freezers, place them on counters to have them dissolve around me just like you.

Just like you, the stranger at the party and the girl who took my hand, stung my palm with a kiss. We crossed our legs opposite each other.
Another. I watched the blood make a small swirl from your left nostril, gather in her perfect teardrop philtrum. She let it stay there, stared at me hard in the bathtub.
My legs were drunk; my head, though,
was sure it was looking at you.

I am better now. I run across overpasses as trains rush through underneath, trying to make them holler their horns. Trick them to think I could jump or fall. Cruel, I know. Just like you.

I don't think of you much when I leave the city.
These days, you come to me when I miss the last train home.
When it rains in August.
When someone wants to pick a fight on the night bus. When I have been drinking and I have to squint one eye to see the stops properly and it makes our town look pretty but exaggerated. That's when I can feel your laugh splinter the skin at the back of my throat.

I have let the guilt of not crying about you anymore replace the burnt skin in my stomach – swallowed from my own mouth, the day they burnt your body. The rest of us stood outside as my nose filled with ash. I felt myself imitating you on a night out but couldn't clear the charred taste for months.

Sometimes I throw a coin over the side of a bridge for luck, or something. Just when I remember how you used to put a penny on your tongue to rid yourself of the chemical flavour that

trickled down your neck.
You said how dirty pennies are.

But what doesn't kill you, right?

This only makes you forever the cross luck bandit. Someone who left as quickly as they had been. Gunslinger with the crushed bullets.
I know I do this now for me, but it still feels like you. You and your charming disease.

Hoarding

At times my heart will run

like the old vacuum cleaner

that my parents still keep in their cellar.

When I go home

I am grateful

that my parents don't carelessly

throw things away.

Home Is a Foreign Fruit

I am afraid that one day I will call home and no one will answer.

I am scared that the word home will become a lost sound.

I worry that one day no one will recognise me as theirs.

In a building that didn't hold me or feel like welcome

I would buy plantain from the local grocery and fry it alone,

eat it on my bed in silence and think about what home used to
   mean to me,

about how foreign these women made me feel.

Put each piece to my mouth and know Ghana,
small, hot and slightly salted on my lips.

I am the child who refused to eat yam;
jollof always tastes strange when it isn't

the way my mother makes it.

I should go back to my parents' house more.
I know that my old houses have lost flavour,

the walls are as grey as the culture within them
and I wonder if anyone will find the small god

of my mother's heart that I stored under the cupboard the day
   I moved out,

wrapped carefully around the pan I left deliberately.

When they cook dead things and add no spices
will anyone think of the little ritual now gone?

Slicing the not-quite-banana up and adding salt.
People put it to their tongues and sang,

Oh, I didn't ever expect it to taste like this!
and they never do.

When homesickness strikes, I will travel to buy ripe plantain and
    take it to my parents' house,

shallow-fry my childhood in a kitchen that smells like rice,
    tomatoes and onions

slow cooking, put a piece of my upbringing to my lips, imagine
    how someone could wear

a continent around their neck, speak in a tongue they
    don't own.

Instead, home is the little quiet in peeling a fruit that English
    people think is meant to be sweet,

adding your heat, oil and salt,
feeling the weight of your family calling you

back to a timeline that you were never absolute on,
plaiting your hair flat to your head, wrapping your wrists red,
    green, yellow and black,

hoping when you call home
someone you love will still answer.

Giant Woman

I wished not to be a giant. The beast formidable and looming. I
wished to be as small as the joy inside me feels these days.
I wanted to make my bones shrink and
my flesh vacuum-tight across the
brittle branches of my spine.
Creaking elbows and delicate wrists.
I wished to be a tiny flower.
Some kind of ethereal creature whose
big opinions fit in
small spaces
when they leave the two
rose petals of my mouth.
I wanted mountains not
to tremble when my heart did.
I wished my grief
to be a beautiful thing and that
in its silence and unsmiling gilt it would be shared and
understood in equal parts
wonderful. I have tried to press myself into the
shape of the little women
around me, ignoring
the burning in my
lower back from
crumpling
my frame
into a less
frightening
form.
I wished
for a
smooth
finish.
Now
I check
the phantom pain in
my neck every morning for the Frankenstein bolts that I have
been given. All those open spaces have tiny
doors
that black
women

with large grief
and loud pain
cannot fit through.
Letting people kick me in
the heart and head, worrying
about how my gut-wrench howl
scares the townsfolk.
I wonder about the pitchforks, the lit torches my open mouth
invited. How many more times I can be chased out the other side
of these city peaks. How someone always needs to be the bad
dog, a rabid thing that has to be put down by the bravest person
in the village.
I may have spent too much
time trying to shrink.
Running to the hills,
praying to be changed
into something less scary.
The abominable creature of anger,
the monster in the hills. Crying great big bodies of liquid into
enormous hands that turn into the rivers that people drink from.
They take huge gulps from their cups and say in between,
Don't go into the forest, a great savage lives there and they'll
devour you whole.
We chased them away a long time ago.
Though every now and then
might quietly question
why the water here
makes everyone
so sad.

I will break
myself

down

each night
wishing

not to be any
person's

giant.

Sing This on the Bad Days

Just let me go.
I am no good anymore.

Some days don't belong to me, they leave me in small deliberate pieces. They split and spill so fast I don't need to shake off the residue. My chest drums like the foot of a very small rabbit and I chase things out of nightmares that leave me in five-day bouts of insomnia. They're beating in the back of my throat now. Maybe it's not the sound of simple anxiety; maybe it is something altogether more unholy than that.

Just take me home.
I need to be alone for a while.

Some days, the bed seems the only suitable place to have me, even though it's the place where the slickest of betrayals have held me.
The hands that live on my shoulders hold my face to the pillows and the dead things gather under my sheets. Some days, the bed really is the only thing that can keep me and I call traitor to the morning, part of me shamefully despairing that my body even woke up again at all.

My head is busted into two and
my heart dismantles for you.

Some days everything is sharp.
Even music will cut into my head and I will bleed from my ears whilst everything around me turns to white noise. I huff the poison from all my bad thoughts. On days like this everyone looks as if they have serrated edges. I bump into them on purpose and cradle the wounds like babies.

These are days of no bandages. These are days of cracked clay. I lay my hate down on my unmade bed and make love to it until it stops making any noise.

My soul is cut and disproved.
I am just no use.

Some days, I feel I am disappearing altogether.
Parts of me fall away; I am left a ribless torso.
I bend and curse and dissolve. I wait for a time when my mind
can piece itself back together, in an order more liveable than this
one.

We Name Hurricanes After People

When they said a hurricane was coming to town,
the buildings still stood.

No brick and metal mountains bowed to the will of any Gale;
                              they said this one went
by another lady's name anyway.

People here still dig for silver on the roads,
but only when the weather warnings come out.

I feel an ancient heart has come along with this wind.
Whips a heartless joy into my cheeks,

pulling at the clothes I wear,
not right for this type of outside, not today.

I heard a man opened his truck door and it came clean off;
                              the trees have been
abandoning themselves – keeling over.

This trouble came into town with just the right amount of force
to make the trees feel

they could fall down and stay there.

They closed the shops in central.
Blue ribbon rung the underpasses in the centres

that stand on riversides like snow globes,
the glass looking weak and willing.

The weather is weeping,
                              pushing people
over,
stropping.

It has lost something and it feels like it knows it today.

They tell me she will have passed through here
by the end of the night,

                    that by tomorrow morning the
only way you could know she was here at all is by what was
ruined on her way through.

                    That's the thing about extreme weather;
no matter the damage, it can't last forever.

If I were a hurricane I would lick the streets
with my angry howl, strip the city to the bone.
Leave nothing upright.

To think grief is like a hurricane,
we give them names
                so when a wild wind comes to town it feels like
          that's all that is left of them.

The Search to Be Good

You lowered your guns for someone who made your face a pincushion for their needle-like fists.

A decade later your mouth will still leak from the holes. When you meet them again, smile.
Act like you are waterproof.

/ Tell your heart it's not a punk or a sucker /

The woman you cradled in to soothe her chaos ran from you so fast, you will see cartoon smoke outlines of her in all the people you love after the fact.

She will reach out to tell you she is happy now. Healthy, settled down with a man and a cat. That hello will always remind you of being robbed of a real goodbye.

/ Tell her you are glad for her joy /

You will always love those who give you their promises like second-hand clothing.

Those whose stories turn you into a stranger in your own home.

/ Go gratefully with the ghost of your friendship /

Smile, because it may be the only language of you they can still speak.

There are moments when a laugh just won't cut it. There is too much cracked love riding on your back.

When teeth act like small tombstones resting in the shallow grave of a grin. When there is nothing sacred in misplaced tenderness,

remember that goodness is a practice and not a given.

/ That is a learned thing I am looking for /

Polaroid

I would like to fold myself

into your camera.

You and I both know that I am

as disposable as a roll of film

and I've captured something beautiful in you,

pressed onto me

through your lens,

that you can come back to

any time

to sift through me

and reminisce.

A Recall of Red, Adolescence on a South London Estate and Other Painful Things in Four Parts

1.

We used to curl up in the first room, on the right-hand side of a third-floor estate. The walls were red. Theatre curtain red, Louis Vuitton bottom heel red, the red on the inside of the cloak of a vampire costume. Red. Talked about our bodies and how we weren't sure of why we wanted to put them against other bodies but we do. Talked of sweet and earnest fingers and wet tongues. The girls we were being, not the girls we knew we were. This week, again, I thought about the ruse Imogen played on my behalf. How I spent the night at a boy's house in Hampton. Told my parents I was in her kitchen, plans cooked up in after-college conceptions. How they didn't believe me, so insisted on picking me up the next morning. My mother in the shotgun seat, bullets in her mouth. My friend covered for me no question, with her girlfriend of then sleepy curled up cat-like in the bedroom. When I had come back from out of town, the night I spent unable to give myself over to a boy two years older than me. I still had his bubble-gum scent on my face, his smoke stuck in my clothes. I put Imogen's perfume on in her room to cover my innocent night evidence with teenage body spray and mint. I'd caught the train back at 8am, convinced myself I'd done the right thing. Climbed into the back seat of my father's car and hoped I didn't have to do too much of my own convincing.

2.
It's the little thought. The devil in it that rolls out new floorboards
for things that we would rather not be thinking of.

How death has been putting its mouth on me since I was a
smaller child,

breathing soot into my unwilling oesophagus, so sometimes
now when I cough my fists come up to cover my mouth and
they get coal rot black.

Dirty,
like I have been running my palms along the underside of cars.

Thinking I still don't know if I will be next,
that perhaps that should terrify me and how it doesn't.

Only at the centre of this new adulthood saturated with
nostalgia, memories are pressed into the lining of old clothes

you just can't throw away because of the tales that come stitched
in them. Skin cells once worked in.

The kid who lived between those threads.

3.

You never knew such things would become these kinds of stories. How Maya's flat always smelt like something was cooking when it often wasn't. That we spent summers inside a circumference of these stacked-up Stockwell blocks. How I hated the boys they befriended teasing us for being the tall girls. I ran my mouth off often, jealous that Imogen's mum let her have parties where boys and girls pressed against each other, desperate for something they had no understanding of. The first in our group to love another woman against the fear of that want that I held in me. How she made it look so easy. Sticky sweet selves we took so seriously, sweaty awkward bumping we wouldn't get in trouble for. The heartache her mother wore then, nothing at all compared to the one she would later wrap around herself. I think she painted the kitchen ceiling blue, if I can remember it right. How art desperately needed to be in that home, so much it escaped from all the hands of the women of the house, slapping itself onto walls. How her little sister would scrawl badly noted rap lyrics, protest in Adidas trackies, whilst the sour-tempered pet rabbit hid underneath her bed. The mix tapes she made of PJ Harvey and the B-52s. It's the little things. That a week ago I heard 'Planet Claire' come on the radio in an overpriced coffee shop the hell worst side of town to me, and I burst into tears at the counter, not understanding why.

4.
And isn't that just the way of things?

some new friend will say in this moment
draped on a kitchen table or a bar,
sucking at the meaning of your memories like

the tar from a cigarette.

You will roll your eyes back into your head, open a window to
try

and get rid of some of the smoke,

think about how you don't have room left in your head for small
    moments from big people

who disappear slowly

and somehow all at once.

Brighton

There is
something rattling
around in my chest, a marble
rolling around the small space
of a thimble. I look to the left of me
on this dark and drunk tin-can
train on track back
to the city we still
call family.
This one
is asleep.
Calm and still,
rescue remedy,
he still smells like the sea.
Unlucky sailor who carries
my secrets. My music trickles
into something new and he stirs a little.
Got a nice gentle shuffle every
few minutes now. I have
to remember
to wake us
when we are
close to London.
I run a bubble gum
around the roof of my mouth,
trying to get the last sweetness out.
I don't know it yet,
but months from this moment
the town I come from will feel like an exit wound.
Cheap wine will look like blood,
all the sugar bowls
needing to be
refilled.
Crumbs I cared about
under the table of the place
where I learned how not to be hungry.
We talked of ions, salt. Let the sea

spit at us, let the pebbles punch
the soles of our feet like
cheap foot-shaped
punching bags.
We put them
in the sea
anyway, knowing
how it freezes, because
you can't visit the ocean
without putting some of your skin to it.
Talked like we always do about how much
better everything would be
if we could love here or
anywhere with a shore.
He looked at me
as if he'd drunk
a fistful
of the stones,
luck suddenly feeling
like a small smooth edge
that sinks when thrown in.
One earphone out, there's a soft snore
escaping him and he's bobbing
like a lost buoy at sea.
Little drift leaning
on me like always,
I shake him
gently.
We are pulling
back into the station.
We are back in our start,
our backyard cage for cardinals.
Small spaces,

small chest,

small breath,

for now.

Good Earth

This area is underprivileged.
The ladies-who-lunch say.
The boys with sports bags.
Sit on signs outside.
The broken walls.
The knickknacks spilling onto the street.
The music never stops.
The neighbours tell ghost stories.
On well-lit front doorsteps.
To rattle the new bones.
Someone is always feeding the birds.
Outside the café.
The one that never closes.
The kids walk back and forth to school.
The church is always shut.
The dog across the street.
Always trying to give kisses to strangers.
The sirens run along the skull of the roads.
The library.
Looks like it might be out of fiction soon.
The door numbers are painted on.
Some streets here don't go to bed.
Someone is always awake.
The groceries compete.
Wave odd-shaped dirt-covered fruit.
There isn't a Wi-Fi hotspot for miles.
But at sundown.
Someone is always frying plantain.
Ackee.
Callaloo.
Salted fish. Yam.
Some type of stew.
It smells like good earth.
The graffiti is left up.
Everyone uses the alleyway to get home.
Trains run slowly.
Sometimes not at all.

The doctor's.
Is run by women in headscarves.
No one is screaming in the waiting rooms.
The dialects bounce off the walls.
Rubbish is collected.
A different time each week.
The night bus is always full to the brim.
The posters on the high road never change.
The ladies-who-lunch hide away.
They are waiting. For the cavalry.
The pavements will be undone one day.
Someone will paint over the effigy of Jesus.
Watching Netflix.
A Starbucks will open.
The café will finally flip the closed sign.
It will smell like brioche. Smoked salmon.
No one will invite you to buy vegetables.
Someone will write a review.
Call it up and coming.
And no one will think of the sky. Opening.
The teeth of the place. Ground down.
Hair pulled back off the face.
They will say it isn't scary anymore.
Because it will look just like everywhere else.

January

When the next wave of grief comes to greet you, and it will, make sure that you have taken a small amount of sugar for under your tongue.

The sour and the weeping will be relentless.

Rub your chest warm again and bury the bad thoughts that come with this cold. Somewhere your feet won't walk over anyone.

Remember that this is solitary and bold.

Take it for walks and hydrate it often, not letting anything but the small sweet in your mouth come out.

It is only a matter of time and no one person can save you from this. You heard someone call it little death once

and they were right.

Acknowledgements

The poem 'Brown Sugar on White Canvas' was first published in the Spoken Word London *Anti-Hate* Anthology in February 2019.

I would like to thank Burning Eye Books and everyone in the team for giving me this opportunity to publish my first collection, as without all of their work this wouldn't be possible. In the same vein I have to thank everyone who has ever come in and out of my life in love in any way. There are countless people to name, but, to mention a few, thank you to my family, both chosen and given, and the poets who have lent their ears and eyes to my work. Thanks in particular to Sara Hirsch, who gave an endless amount of support, inspiration, time and expertise to help shape this book and bring it to life, to Harry Tewkesbury, for keeping joy in abundance with me from the offset and throughout this process, and certainly to Imogen Goldie, who was the first person to write me a poem and to read one I had written.

I am so grateful for all of you.

Lightning Source UK Ltd.
Milton Keynes UK
UKHW012115180620
365223UK00005B/306